Rest in Peace

First published in 1997 in Great Britain by
Kevin Mayhew Ltd, Rattlesden, Bury St Edmunds,
Suffolk IP30 0SZ

ISBN 1 84003 102 6
Catalogue No 1500158

Printed and bound in Great Britain

Acknowledgements

Bible quotations are taken from the *New Jerusalem
Bible*, published by Darton, Longman and Todd,
1985, and the *New International Version*, © Copyright
1973, 1978, 1984 by International Bible Society,
published by Hodder & Stoughton Ltd.
All rights reserved.

Extracts from The Funeral Service from
The Alternative Service Book 1980, © The Central
Board of Finance of the Church of England, are
reproduced by permission.

Contents

PART ONE *Reflection*

Comfort and hope   4

The Christian understanding of death   4

Some prayers for personal use   6

Some words from Scripture   6

After the funeral   7

PART TWO *Action*

A step-by-step guide of what to do after a death   8

Funeral arrangements   9

A step-by-step guide to what happens on the day of the funeral   11

The role of the funeral director   13

The role of the minister   13

PART THREE *Helpful Information*

Hymns suitable for funerals   15

Bible readings suitable for funerals and for personal use   15

Useful names, addresses and publications   15

A FINAL PRAYER   16

xt: Susan Hardwick

ver and watercolour illustrations: Katie Millard

esign and typesetting: Jaquetta Sergeant

EASE NOTE: Both ordained people and specially
ensed lay people can take funerals in the Church of
gland, and so the term 'minister' is used in this
ok to indicate the person who will officiate at the
eral service.

ateful thanks to David Devall, MBIE, MBIF,
pFD, DipFSM, Managing Director, D. B. Devall,
mily Funeral Directors, Nuneaton, Warwickshire,
his advice in the preparation of this book.

Comfort and Hope

Whether anticipated, prepared and planned for, or unexpected and sudden, the death of a loved one is usually devastating.

However foreseen, nothing can totally prepare those closest for the feelings they experience.

Numbness; shock; disbelief; deep grief; anger at God, the doctors and nurses, or at the injustice of it all; feelings of guilt for what was not done for the deceased; denial; relief that she or he is finally out of pain – these are just some of the very usual feelings experienced at the death of a loved one, and for a long time after.

They do not happen in any neat order or pattern, for we will each react in our own individual and unique way. We have to be gentle with ourselves at this time, giving ourselves permission for these turbulent feelings which will most probably repeat themselves many times over the succeeding weeks, months and maybe even years, before we can declare ourselves truly healed.

We can, though, be assured of God's nearer presence and that, when we call upon him, he will support and sustain us with his strength and his love.

> The eternal God is your refuge,
> and underneath are the everlasting arms.
> *Deuteronomy 33:27*

> Jesus said, 'Blessed are those who mourn,
> for they will be comforted'.   *Matthew 5:4*

> When the Lord saw her, his heart went out
> to her and he said, 'Don't cry'.   *Luke 7:13*

The Christian Understanding of Death

> For I am certain of this: neither death nor life,
> nor angels, nor principalities,
> nothing already in existence and
> nothing still to come,
> nor any power, nor the heights nor the depths,
> nor any created thing whatever,
> will be able to come between us and
> the love of God,
> known to us in Christ Jesus our Lord.

So wrote Paul (in Romans 8:38, 39). Paul was a leader of the Early Christian Church, who knew tragedy, fear and heartache and yet, all along, also knew the constancy of God's love supporting and sustaining and strengthening him.

The Christian view and understanding of death actually finds its roots in the mystery of life and of a God who has not only created this amazing world we live in and everything within it, but who also enters intimately into all that he has brought into being.

The Book of Genesis draws a wonderful picture of the relationship between God the Father and the children he has conceived and created. God calls to them to walk with him in the garden he has made for them.

All through the Bible, God's continuous love and care are stressed, as he reveals himself more and more fully. He speaks to Moses in the Burning Bush declaring his identity: 'I Am'.

Finally, in the birth and life of Jesus he makes himself incarnate and human; as one who suffers with and for humankind, and who brings healing and wholeness.

Through his death and resurrection, Jesus showed us the path back to God. When he burst out of his tomb on that first Easter morning – for mere earthly rock could not contain him – he proved that nothing, but *nothing*, could limit his love and that death had lost its sting for ever.

In the words of an Easter prayer, often used at funerals:

Father, we give you thanks, because through Jesus
you have given us the hope of a glorious resurrection;
so that, although death comes to us all,
yet we rejoice in the promise of eternal life;
for to your faithful people life is changed, not taken away;
and when our mortal flesh is laid aside,
an everlasting dwelling place is made ready for us in heaven.

A Preface to the Resurrection for use in Eucharistic Prayers (ASB)

John, a close friend of Jesus and one of his disciples, recorded Jesus as saying, 'No one can have greater love than to lay down their life for their friends' (John 15:13 adapted). Jesus literally lost his life for our sakes, in order that we may find our way back to God. By his death he has destroyed death and opened up a pathway to eternal life.

What happens after we die remains a mystery. We are told everyone will be judged by God, and the relationship between God's love and his judgement and mercy is one of the constant themes of Christian writing.

What is heaven like? Jesus gave us some hints, but we cannot know too precisely; it is probably beyond our ability to imagine, even in our wildest dreams. Suffice it to say, there we shall be delighting in the presence of God and his love, and the whole company of heaven. If that is heaven, then hell must be a state in which we are separated from that love of God. How we live our earthly lives must affect how we can experience God. However, God's grace has the power to transform even the darkest of lives.

5

Some Prayers for Personal Use

Dear God,
please help me.
This awful pain is impossible to bear.
Amen.

Loving Saviour,
I come to you just as I am,
with no pretence, no bravery.
I lay before you my grief and my tears,
my worries, my fears and all the confusion
and pain of these dark days.
Please help me to carry the burden
and to bear it all.
May your peace reign in my heart and my life.
Amen.

Holy Lord,
most holy and life-giving Lord,
breathe your Spirit into my deadened soul
that I may live again.
Amen.

Dear God,
the funeral day is here.
The cars are waiting, but I'm reluctant to go
to that final goodbye.
Jesus, stay very close.
Give me the strength I need to get through it.
Amen.

Jesus,
please give me the strength to face the day
and all whom I shall meet
with a calm spirit;
to look and to see with your eyes.
When people stumble out their sympathy
may I listen with your ears,
and may I have the grace to remember
that they might need comforting, too.
Help me to tread gently through my world today –
your world – and please will you walk beside me?
Amen.

Some Words from Scripture

God said, 'As a mother comforts a child, so I shall comfort you
Isaiah 66:1

God is near to the brokenhearted, he helps those whose spirit i
crushed.
Psalm 34:1

When I was brought low, God gave me strength. My heart, be a
peace once again.
Psalm 116:6b-7

Jesus said, 'Come to me, all you who are weary and burdened,
and I will give you rest'.
Matthew 11:2

For this is how God loved the world: he gave his only Son, so
that everyone who believes in him may not perish but may hav
eternal life.
John 3:1

Jesus said, 'Do not let your hearts be troubled. You trust in God
trust also in me. In my Father's house, there are many places to
live in . . .'
John 14:1, 2

Jesus came and stood among them. He said to them, 'Peace be
with you'.
John 20:1

After the Funeral

Those who have lost a loved one can be so busy with the practical details and arrangements necessary immediately after the death that the full impact of their loss may not be experienced for some time.

At the beginning of this book are listed some of the very normal and usual feelings experienced by the bereaved. Coming to terms with the loss of a loved one is like a journey containing within it many different stages. The amount of time required to go through each stage will vary from person to person, and each stage will probably be re-covered several times: things we think we have come to terms with at one level of our understanding often have to be worked through again at deeper levels before we can truly say we are healed of our loss. Maybe – indeed, very probably – at one level or another the marks of sorrow will never totally disappear.

However, just as the eternal wounds of the nails and of the crown of thorns are signs of Jesus' love, so our scars are signs of our loving: like the scars of Jesus, they are signs of glory.

When wounds heal, scars are formed. But God sees them, not as blemishes, but as marks of his glory.

Mother Julian of Norwich, a famous medieval mystic

There does come a time when we feel we both want and need to turn from the graveside in order to move forward into the future. The death of someone we love points up vividly both how fragile and how precious is the gift of life; a precious gift to be used to the very best of our ability. In the words of a prayer from the ASB funeral service:

Grant us, Lord, the wisdom and the grace
to use aright the time that is left to us here on earth.
Lead us to repent of our sins,
the evil we have done and the good we have not done;
and strengthen us to follow the steps of your Son,
in the way that leads to the fullness of eternal life;
through Jesus Christ our Lord. Amen.

A Step-by-step Guide of What to Do after a Death

1   *When the death is expected and occurs in the home*

    a   Contact the doctor of the deceased.

    b   The doctor will give you a medical certificate stating the cause of death.

    c   Contact your preferred funeral director and, if you wish, your local minister. Otherwise, if you prefer, the funeral director will make the contact for you.

    d   Before making firm arrangements for the funeral:

       i   Check where the money is coming from to pay for the funeral.

       ii   Find out if there is a will, since this may give requests and instructions about the funeral arrangements.

    e   Contact the registrar and arrange to visit the registrar's office. (Ask what certification and documents you are required to take with you.) The registrar will give you a certificate of registration and a certificate of disposal.

2   *When the death is unexpected and occurs in the home*

    a   Contact the deceased's doctor immediately.

    b   In the case of accidental, suspicious or violent circumstances, contact the police as well.

    c   The doctor may need to report the death to a coroner and, if this is the case, there will probably be a post-mortem. If the death is due to natural causes, the coroner will issue a form for the registrar. If the death is violent, caused by an accident, or industrial disease, or if the cause of death is still uncertain after a post-mortem, the coroner will hold an inquest.

3   *If the death occurs in hospital*

The nursing staff will tell you what you have to do. The hospital administration department will give you a death certificate if it is clear what is the cause of death. If the death is sudden, or if the cause is uncertain or needs investigating in some way, the doctor may ask permission to carry out a post-mortem. In this situation the doctor will report the death to a coroner.

Normally, at your request, the doctor or the funeral director will contact the appropriate people. Sometimes, though, it should be noted that for various reasons it is not possible to comply with the request. Where a body is used for research or teaching it has to be buried or cremated within two years. In this situation, when the funeral cannot take place within a few days of death, it is a good idea to have a memorial service. A tree, shrub, rose bush or similar could be planted and dedicated to the memory of the deceased, as a focus for the bereaved.

Funeral Arrangements

You would be well advised to choose a funeral director who is a member of the National Association of Funeral Directors (NAFD); also to ask for an estimate of the cost. The funeral director you choose will be able to advise you and give you help in your decisions regarding the funeral. Either they or you will contact your local minister, who will arrange to meet you to talk about the funeral service and to offer support, practical advice, comfort and counselling.

Death marks the close of earthly life, and the funeral is an opportunity for friends and family to gather together to share their memories and all the complex feelings that attend the death of someone who has been a central part of their lives. It is also an important part of the process of coming to terms with the reality of the death.

There is a variety of options with regard to both the venue of the service, and its content. Your funeral director will be able to advise you about the full range of possibilities, including non-Christian forms of committal.

Venue

Generally, you may choose from the following:

a   A service in church, followed by burial in a cemetery, or cremation and interment of ashes. After a church service, many families choose that the cremation or burial be restricted to family, and maybe very close friends, only.

b   A service in a crematorium chapel, followed by the burial or distribution/scattering of ashes at a later date. Sometimes it is decided that the funeral service will be a private affair for just the family, and maybe very close friends as well, to be followed by a thanksgiving or memorial service at a later date. This can be a very helpful alternative, especially if large numbers of people are involved.

Planning the service

If you would like to participate in the planning of the service, the minister will be happy to advise you. There are also some suggestions listed on page 15 of hymns and Bible readings. On the other hand, if you wish to have as little to do with the planning as possible, and to leave it all to the minister, this is also quite acceptable.

Those responsible for the conduct of the funeral will be anxious that the service is as meaningful as possible and reflects the wishes of the bereaved, so you should feel free to discuss what you would like the funeral to contain. Whilst, if it is to be a Christian service, it has to have certain elements, there are many ways in which you can contribute.

For example:

1 Choosing a reading – from the Bible, or another religious or secular book, or a poem.
2 Choosing the hymns.
3 Writing some prayers.
4 Saying a few words about the deceased in the service.
5 Sharing with the minister important aspects of the deceased's life, their personality and character, special instances that reflect these, in order that s/he can give a meaningful address at the funeral.
6 Providing a tape with a song or some music that is particularly meaningful, or which reminds you of the deceased. This is often good played near the end, just before the final prayers, or as exit music.
7 If one of the mourners is musical, perhaps s/he would like to sing or play an appropriate piece of music.

At the graveside

In some areas it is customary for the mourners to file past, each taking a small handful of earth from that beside the grave, and scattering it onto the coffin.

If asked (some make it their custom to do it anyway), the minister will take flowers from the main wreaths and give one

to each of the chief mourners to cast into the grave. If this is what you would like to happen, tell the minister and s/he will be happy to accommodate you.

Flowers – or donations in lieu?

Money to a charity It is often the choice of mourners that money should be sent to a charity they name instead of flowers being given. Your funeral director will be happy to advise you. Many funeral directors will also collect charity donations on your behalf.

A Step-by-step Guide to What Happens on the Day of the Funeral

Before the funeral

1   The body of the deceased normally lies in the chapel of rest at the funeral director's until the day of the funeral. Some families like to have the body at their home for a period of time before the funeral.

   Occasionally the family request that the body lies in church overnight prior to the funeral, with candles surrounding the coffin. Prior permission would be needed from the minister.

2   With regard to the funeral cars there is a variety of options:
   a   Cars from funeral director's directly to the church/crematorium/cemetery, and the family make their own way to the venue.
   b   Hearse to church/crematorium/cemetery. Car sent from funeral director's to collect family (those who do not want to follow the hearse) and take to venue.
   c   The family meet at the funeral director's and then go as a cortege to the venue.
   d   Hearse and car/s go to the house to collect the family and take to church/crematorium/cemetery. (This is the most usual.)

At the church – the usual procedure

The detailed contents of the service will obviously depend upon what has been arranged between the minister and the family. The basic framework is set out below.

   When the cars arrive at the church the minister meets the funeral cortege, and walks ahead of the coffin and bearers which

11

are followed by the mourners. As the procession enters the church, those already inside stand.

Passages from scripture are said as the procession goes down the aisle, and people go to their respective places. Everyone sits for a Bible reading, after which the minister will give a short address. This is usually followed by a hymn and the prayers. A second hymn may then be sung, followed by the minister commending the deceased to the mercy of God. There may be a final hymn, or piece of music, during which the funeral procession leaves church led by the minister, followed by the coffin, then the chief mourners, then the rest of the congregation.

The committal
Burial

The funeral procession proceeds to the cemetery. When the mourners are gathered around the grave, the coffin is lowered in. The minister reads the verses from Scripture that are set, followed by the prayer of committal. At the words 'earth to earth, ashes to ashes, dust to dust', s/he will usually scatter some earth onto the coffin.

After, there is time for people to look at the flowers that have been sent, before leaving.

Cremation

The funeral procession proceeds to the crematorium. The form of service is as for burial. At the words 'we now commit his/her body to be cremated', curtains come across so that the coffin is no longer on view. This is a powerfully emotional moment for many people.

Burial of ashes

This is normally arranged to take place a day or two after the cremation. The funeral director collects the ashes from the crematorium, and meets the mourners at the site of the proposed burial of ashes. The service is very short and simple. The casket, or the ashes on their own, are placed in the burial place and the service consists of just a few short prayers.

After-funeral reception

People often travel some distance to attend a funeral and if it is possible to offer some sort of simple hospitality, it is much appreciated. It is an opportunity for sharing in all sorts of ways and it can also ease the time immediately after the funeral. A number of funeral directors now offer facilities to arrange catering for these occasions.

The Role of the Funeral Director

'Funerals should be as individual as we are individual ourselves. So far as is possible, anything that is helpful for the families should be done.' (David Devall, funeral director)

1 *Technical Adviser* – registration and certificates required; the DHSS system; local customs re burials, headstones, etc.
2 *Contractor* – family contracts coffin, use of premise, chapel of rest, interview room, mortuary, hearses, etc.
3 *Agent for family* – can arrange minister, church, death notice, floral tributes, order of service, catering, etc.
4 *Custodian of deceased* – last offices (washing, preparing the body), facilities for viewing, etc.
5 *Master of Ceremonies* – leads family through procedure of funeral step by step.

N.B. If you have a particular wish, do let your funeral director know, and they will try to accommodate you.

An example: Seven-year-old Greg loved fire engines, and so his parents asked if the route to the church for his funeral could go via the fire station. The funeral director phoned the fire station officer with the result that, when the funeral cortege passed, all the fire engines were out on the forecourt washed and polished, with all the fire-fighters in full uniform and standing to attention. The cars slowed down as they passed, the fire-fighters saluted and the sirens were sounded.

Greg also loved the colour orange. Those attending the service had been asked if they could try to wear something orange. Hats, scarves, dresses, shirts were found by the mourners with the result that the church positively glowed with Greg's favourite colour.

The Role of the Minister

1 To arrange and conduct the funeral service in a way that is as meaningful as possible for the mourners.
2 To minister to the needs of the bereaved; to support, comfort, console and link together both grief and hope.

3 S/he makes a pre-funeral visit to the family where possible t
be alongside them in their sadness and bewilderment and,
hopefully, to help the family cope with and work through
some of the initial stages of the grief process. It is also a tim
to discuss the funeral, answer questions, and to discover
what might be said about the deceased in the funeral
address: the principal facts and significant points about thei
character and personality and life.

4 To help the bereaved explore faith questions, for example:
'Why?' 'How could a loving God allow this to happen?' 'Li
after death', and so on.

5 To be a person to whom the bereaved can turn at any time
for emotional support and to help them work through the
grieving process.

Hymns Suitable for Funerals

O Love, that wilt not let me go

Do not be afraid

Abide with me

Be still, for the presence of the Lord

Dear Lord and Father of mankind

I cannot tell how he, whom angels worship

I heard the voice of Jesus say

Within our darkest night

Lead us, heavenly Father, lead us

Be still, my soul

The day thou gavest, Lord, is ended

The King of love my shepherd is

Faithful vigil ended

The Lord's my shepherd

Be still and know that I am God

Jerusalem the golden

In heavenly love abiding

Rock of ages, cleft for me

All of these hymns may be found in most
hymn books

Bible Readings Suitable for Funerals and for Personal Use

Psalms: 20; 23; 24; 42; 43; 46; 61; 63; 84; 91; 103; 116; 121; 130; 139; 142; 146

Job 19:25-27

Isaiah 25:6-9; 40:1-11; 61:1-3

Ezekiel 36:26-28

Matthew 11:28-30

Mark 5:22-24, 35-43; 10:13-16; 15:33-39; 16:1-6

Luke 7:11-17; 23:33, 39-43; 24:13-35

John 6:35-40; 10:11-15; 11:17-27; 12:23-28; 14:1-6; 17:24-26

Acts 10:34-43

Romans 5:1-8; 6:3-11; 8:14-25; 8:31-39; 14:7-9

1 Corinthians 13:4-13; 15:35-43; 15:51-57

2 Corinthians 1:2-5; 4:7-18

Ephesians 3:14-21

Philippians 3:8-16

1 Thessalonians 4:13-18

Hebrews 10:19-25

1 John 3:1-3

Revelation 7:9-17; 21:1-7

Useful Names, Addresses and Publications

The Compassionate Friends

53 North Street, Bristol BS23 1EN. Tel: Helpline 0117 953 9639; Administration: 0117 966 5202
Friendship and understanding for bereaved parents

Cruse Bereavement Care

(Branches nationwide) National Office: Cruse House, 126 Sheen Road, Richmond, Surrey
TW9 1UR. Tel: 0181 940 4818
Counselling and advice for all bereaved people

Department of Social Security

(Branches nationwide) See phonebook for your local office
Produce a free 60-page booklet 'What to do after a death' (No. D49) – very helpful and comprehensive

Lifelines for the Bereaved by Susan Hardwick, published by Kevin Mayhew Ltd, 1997
One of a series of eight little booklets for people in particular life situations

A Final Prayer

Lord,
as I rise from the dark dead time of bereavement,
help me to live the years left fully, until the day comes
for me to face my own death
in the sure and certain hope of resurrection to eternal life,
and that I shall be coming home to you:
my Saviour, my Redeemer, my Lord. Amen.